All about...

Roald Dahl

Heinemann
LIBRARY

Vic Parker

www.heinemann.co.uk/library
Visit our website to find out more information about **Heinemann Library** books.

To order:
 Phone 44 (0) 1865 888066
 Send a fax to 44 (0) 1865 314091
 Visit the Heinemann Bookshop at www.heinemann.co.uk/library to browse our catalogue and order online.

First published in Great Britain by Heinemann Library, Halley Court, Jordan Hill, Oxford OX2 8EJ, part of Harcourt Education. Heinemann is a registered trademark of Harcourt Education Ltd.

Editorial: Lucy Thunder and Helen Cannons
Design: David Poole and Geoff Ward
Picture Research: Rebecca Sodergren and Kay Altwegg
Production: Edward Moore

Originated by Ambassador Litho Ltd
Printed and bound in Hong Kong, China by South China Printing

ISBN 0 431 17981 6
07 06 05 04 03
10 9 8 7 6 5 4 3 2 1

British Library Cataloguing in Publication Data
Parker, Vic
Dahl, Roald. – (All About...)
823.9'14
A full catalogue record for this book is available from the British Library.

Acknowledgements
The Publishers would like to thank the following for permission to reproduce photographs:
Jan Baldwin Photography p**17**; Sharna Balfour/Gallo Images/Corbis p**11**; Quentin Blake p**25**; Camera Press pp**5** (Frank Herrmann), **27** (Simon Sykes); Disney Enterprises, Inc. p**15**; Ronald Grant Archive pp**20**, **21**, **23**; James Hawkins Photography p**29**; Chris Honeywell pp**18**, **19**, **22**, **28**; Hulton Archive pp**7**, **8**, **16**; Museum of Flight/Corbis p**12**; North Somerset Museum p**9**; Photo Library Wales p**6**; Popperfoto p**14**; Repton School p**10**; Topham Picturepoint p**24**.

Cover photograph of Roald Dahl at a book signing in November 1989, reproduced with permission of ABL/Rex Features.

The Publishers would like to thank Stephen Noon for his assistance in the preparation of this book.

Every effort has been made to contact copyright holders of any material reproduced in this book. Any omissions will be rectified in subsequent printings if notice is given to the Publishers.

Sources
The author and Publishers gratefully acknowledge the publications which were used for research and as written sources for this book:

Boy, Roald Dahl (Jonathan Cape, 1983) p**9**
Going Solo, Roald Dahl (Jonathan Cape, 1986)
The New York Times, obituary by William H. Honan (24 November 1990) p**27 bottom**
Roald Dahl, Haydn Middleton (Heinemann Library, 1998) pp**10**, **13**, **25**
Roald Dahl, Jeremy Treglown (Faber and Faber, 1994) pp**23**, **26 bottom**
Roald Dahl, Mark I. West (Twayne, 1992) p**27 top**
The Sunday Times, article by Tessa Dahl (23 April 2000) p**18**
www.spaghettibookclub.org p**20**

Fiction works by Roald Dahl are cited in the text.

Contents

Any words shown in the text in bold, **like this**, are
explained in the Glossary.

Who was Roald Dahl?

Roald Dahl is possibly the best-loved children's writer of all time. His thrilling tales for grown-ups are also among the finest short stories ever written. Dahl's books have been **published** in 34 different languages and are best-sellers all over the world. They have become readers' favourites in spite of **critics** sometimes not liking them. Several stories have been made into gripping TV dramas and Hollywood movies (although Roald did not always like these versions).

What was Roald Dahl like?

Roald was a fascinating man who had an extremely interesting life. He lived in Africa for a while and flew fighter-planes in **World War II**.

▲ An illustration from one of Roald's most popular books, *Matilda*.

Roald married a Hollywood star, and got to know many famous and talented people along the way. He was very tall and had a big, loud personality to match.

Sometimes people thought he was annoyingly full of himself and boastful. However, most of the time people found Roald Dahl to be as entertaining as his books.

Factfile

★ Date of birth	13 September 1916
★ Star sign	Virgo
★ Nickname	'Apple' because he was the 'apple of his mother's eye'. Nickname as a young adult – 'Lofty' in the **RAF** because he was so tall.
★ Hobbies	Photography and collecting things (as a child he collected conkers and birds' eggs; as an adult he collected art, antiques and wine)
★ Favourite food	Caviar and chocolate, chocolate and more chocolate!
★ Favourite book	*Mr Midshipman Easy* by Captain Frederick Marryat
★ Bad habits	Not always cleaning his fingernails
★ Pet hates	Bullies and his own birthday!

Roald Dahl in his garden at Gipsy House.

Early years

Roald Dahl's parents were both **Norwegian**. His father, Harald, moved to Cardiff in Wales in the 1880s to set up a business as a **ship-broker**. He died when Roald was only three. Roald was brought up by his mother, Sofie, in a village called Llandaff, near Cardiff. He had one older sister (another older sister had died just a few weeks before his father) and two younger sisters.

Alone in a big family

Roald was his mother's only son. Many of the main characters in his stories also grow up on their own in some way. Charlie, in *Charlie and the Chocolate Factory*, has no brothers and sisters. James, in *James and the Giant Peach*, has no brothers and sisters or parents. Matilda does not fit in to her family at all, as they are all horrible!

▲ The Norwegian Seamen's Church in Cardiff. Roald was **baptized** here as a child.

▲ This sweet shop in the 1920s, with its schoolboy customers, is probably quite like the one that was in Llandaff.

Starting school

Roald was six when he began at his first school, Elm Tree House. A year later, he moved to Llandaff Cathedral School. Every day, Roald's journey took him past a marvellous shop filled with delicious sweets. However, the woman who ran the sweet shop was old, bad-tempered and ugly. All the boys thought she was a witch! One day, when she was not looking, Roald put a dead mouse inside a jar of gob-stoppers to scare her. His headmaster found out and gave him a beating as punishment.

Ideas from real life

In Dahl's stories there are plenty of nasty, witch-like women and cruel adults who like to beat children, such as the bullying headteacher, Miss Trunchbull, in *Matilda* and the horrid Aunts Sponge and Spiker in *James and the Giant Peach*. Perhaps the woman in the sweet shop gave Roald **inspiration** for his books!

Going on holiday

Every summer holiday, the Dahls went to visit family in Norway. First they stopped off in the capital city, Oslo. Roald's mother's parents lived there, with two of Roald's aunts. Then the family went to the seaside at a small island called Tjöme. Roald thought of Norway as another home. He loved spending long days fishing and exploring islands in boats. In the dark evenings, his grandmother and aunts told him scary folk tales about witches, giants and trolls.

▲ The streets of Oslo, Norway, in the 1920s. Roald's mother's parents lived here.

Imagining monsters

Gruesome characters from Norwegian stories coloured Roald's imagination all his life. He describes the Bloodbottler giant in *The BFG* like this: 'His skin was reddish-brown ... There was black hair sprouting on his chest and arms ... The eyes were tiny black holes ... But the mouth was huge ... rivers of spit ran down over the chin ... this ghastly brute ate men, women and children every night.'

▲ St Peter's Preparatory School in Western-super-Mare was a large, grand building.

Being a boarder

When Roald was nine, he was sent to a **boarding school** called St Peter's, in Weston-super-Mare in England. Roald was very frightened at first. He had never spent a single night away from his family. To make things worse, Roald found that life at boarding school was very strict. There were lots of rules to follow and the teachers liked to give hard punishments to any boy who broke one. Roald was very **homesick** for a long time. Every week he wrote a long letter to his mother – a habit that he kept up, even as a grown up. He signed his letters simply, 'Boy'.

What Roald said

Roald tried to sound cheery in his letters home from boarding school, even when he felt miserable. This is what his very first letter from St Peter's said, dated 23 September 1925:

'Dear Mama,
I am having a lovely time here. We play football every day here. The beds have no springs. Will you send my stamp album, and quite a lot of swops. The masters are very nice. I've got all my clothes now, and a belt, and tie, and a school jersey.
love from Boy'

Secondary school

When Roald was thirteen, at the same time as his family moved to Kent, he went to another boarding school – Repton in Derbyshire. He liked it even less than St Peter's. He hated the old-fashioned uniform, the teachers were extremely strict and the older boys bullied the younger boys. Also, Roald was not very good at his classwork. Roald's English teacher wrote this on an end-of-term report in 1930: 'I have never met a boy who so persistently [all the time] writes the exact opposite of what he means.'

Tasting pleasure

Yet Roald did enjoy some things. He was excellent at games and loved learning photography. Best of all, the boys sometimes tested new chocolate bars for Cadbury's! Roald began to wonder about the people who invented chocolates and what it might be like inside a chocolate factory...

Roald at Repton School, aged seventeen.

Looking for adventure

Roald longed to travel to distant, strange places. When he left school in 1934, he began a job with Shell Oil Company in London, which he hoped would take him abroad. In 1938 Roald got his wish. The company posted him to an East African country now called Tanzania, to sell oil to businesses there. Roald hugely enjoyed what he later called 'my African adventure'. The only things he didn't like were the deadly snakes!

▲ Roald enjoyed the sights in Tanzania, including Mount Kilimanjaro, shown here.

Roald becomes a fighter pilot

In September 1939, **World War II** broke out. Several countries decided to fight together to stop German armies marching into other people's lands. Roald wanted to help. He joined the **Royal Air Force (RAF)** so he could learn to fly for free! Roald went to Kenya to train as a pilot. He wrote to his mother that he had never enjoyed himself so much.

Dead or alive?

After nearly a year of training, Roald was ordered to join the fighting around Egypt. He had to fly for a whole day to reach the rocky desert where his base was meant to be. However, when Roald reached the spot, he could not find the base.

To make things worse, darkness was falling and his plane was running out of petrol. Roald had no choice but to try an emergency landing in the desert. He had a terrible accident. His plane hit a huge rock, smashed into the sand and burst into flames. Roald was very badly injured. Luckily, he was rescued by some British soldiers and rushed to an Egyptian hospital.

▲ Roald learnt to fly in a 'Tiger Moth' biplane, like this one.

What the RAF said

Roald's fellow pilots nicknamed him Lofty, because he was so tall. He only just squashed inside a tiny fighter-plane's **cockpit**! After the war, the leader of his team said:

'There is no doubt in my mind that Lofty was a very good fighter pilot and very gallant [brave].'

War hero

Roald needed several operations and spent months recovering. Yet he was determined to fly again. As soon as he was well enough, he went to join the war in Greece. This was extremely dangerous because Germany had taken over almost the whole country.

There were only 20 British fighter pilots (including Roald) against 1000 German planes. Roald's team had to fight several air battles every day. In just over a week, more than half of them were killed. Roald managed to destroy several aeroplanes and stay alive. Then he and the remaining pilots were sent to fight over Syria. For four weeks, Roald flew skilfully and bravely, dodging enemy bullets. However, his old crash injuries started to give him bad headaches and **blackouts**. In the summer of 1941, the RAF told Roald he was no longer fit to fly. They sent him home. Roald had not seen his family for three years.

In Roald's own words

You can read more about Roald's daring deeds as a fighter pilot in a book he wrote called *Going Solo*. This follows on from what he wrote about his childhood in *Boy*.

Roald discovers he is a writer

Roald's family had moved to the village of Grendon Underwood in Buckinghamshire. However, he was not at home with them for long. In January 1942, the **RAF** ordered Roald to go to the USA, to work in the British **Embassy** in Washington, D.C.

▲ The British Embassy in the US capital city, Washington, D.C.

Putting pen to paper

Roald's job involved meeting important people and telling them about his exciting wartime adventures. The famous English author C. S. Forester met Roald and wanted to write a story about the dashing young hero. He asked Roald to jot down some notes. However, Roald found it easier to write a proper story instead. Forester thought it was fantastic! He sent it to be **published** in the weekly magazine, the *Saturday Evening Post*.

When the famous English writer
C. S. Forester received Roald's story,
he sent him a letter that ended like this:

'...the Post *is asking if you will write more
stories for them. I do hope you will.
Did you know you were a writer?'*

Roald's first story for children

If Roald had not met C. S. Forester, he might never have
discovered that he had a gift for writing. Now he tried another
story. RAF pilots blamed mischievous elves called Gremlins for
anything that went wrong with their aeroplanes. Roald imagined
what these made-up creatures might be like. He dreamed
up Gremlin girlfriends called Fifinellas and Gremlin children
called Widgets. Then he wrote a
tale for children about them all.

When Roald had finished his story,
he showed it to his bosses. They
thought it would be perfect as a
children's movie, and they sent it
to Walt Disney. Disney loved it,
too, and told his studios to start
work on turning it into a film.
Roald went out to Hollywood to
help. However, the studios could
not decide whether to use actors or
make a cartoon. The movie plans
ground to a halt. Still, in 1943 the
story was published in the USA,
Britain and Australia as Roald's
first book.

The GREMLINS

FROM THE
WALT DISNEY
PRODUCTION

A ROYAL AIR FORCE STORY BY
Flight Lieutenant Roald Dahl

LONDON   COLLINS   GLASGOW

▲ The title page of Roald's first
published book!

Success and sadness

Roald continued to write in his spare time. He went back to writing short stories for adults. By the time the war finished in 1945, he had written sixteen short war stories that appeared in US magazines.

After the war, Roald returned to his family in Buckinghamshire determined to be a full-time writer. It proved much harder than he thought. Suddenly, people did not want to read about the war any more and Roald had to find something else to write about. He started to make up short stories about **characters** who seemed ordinary at first, but turned out to have horrid, dark secrets. English **publishers** thought these chilling tales were too shocking. However, US magazines still wanted to buy them and in 1951 Roald returned to live and write in New York.

▲ Roald's beautiful and famous first wife, the actor Patricia Neal.

Love and money

Roald had many rich, successful friends in the USA. They loved the tall, loud story-teller who entertained them with strange tales. At a party in 1952, Roald met a Hollywood movie star called Patricia Neal. They married in 1953.

Also in 1953, a book of Roald's spine-tingling tales for adults was **published**. It was called *Someone Like You* and was a huge success across the USA. Pat and Roald were one of the most famous couples in the country.

▲ Roald Dahl did much of his writing in the garden at Gipsy House.

Family affairs

In 1955, Pat and Roald had their first baby, a little girl they called Olivia. Over the next few years, the family lived partly in New York and partly in England. They bought a cottage in Great Missenden, Buckinghamshire, near to Roald's mother and sisters. They came to name it Gipsy House. Another daughter, Tessa, was born in 1957 and a son, Theo, in 1960.

Stories for his children

Roald loved being a father. He spent lots of time with his children and made up bedtime stories for them. Roald had another book of creepy stories for adults published, *Kiss Kiss*, but he ran out of ideas for more. So, he decided to write down one of his children's bedtime tales instead. Roald's publisher in the USA liked it and turned it into a book called *James and the Giant Peach*. Roald began to write down another bedtime tale, about a poor boy and a magical chocolate factory.

What about a chocolate factory
That makes fantastic and marvellous
Things — with a crazy man running it?

▲ This scribbled note was Roald's first written idea for his book *Charlie and the Chocolate Factory*.

What Roald's daughter said

Roald encouraged his children to use their imaginations. When Tessa was grown up, she wrote this in an imaginary letter to Roald:

'I awoke one morning to see my name written across our lawn ... you told me the fairies had done it in the night. (Much later I discovered it was you who had sprayed your treasured grass with weed killer.)'

Double disaster

Late in 1960, the family were in New York when something terrible happened. A taxi cab crashed into baby Theo's pram. Theo was very badly injured. Roald decided that the family should move to England for good, so Theo could be treated at a top London hospital. Roald spent lots of time trying to help his son recover. *James and the Giant Peach* was selling well in the USA, but Roald was too busy to do much new writing. He finished off his chocolate factory story and sent it to his publisher. Then, in November 1962, tragedy struck again. Seven-year-old Olivia became ill with measles and suddenly died. Roald was heartbroken. He did not feel like ever writing anything again.

▲ Olivia Dahl's grave in the churchyard at Little Missenden, Buckinghamshire.

Roald's writing creates a storm

Pat tried to get over Olivia's death by throwing herself into her work. The family went to the USA, so she could film a new movie, *Hud*. Roald shut himself away from his family and friends because of his sadness. However, Roald became a little happier in May 1964, when Pat gave birth to another daughter, Ophelia. Then, in September, *Charlie and the Chocolate Factory* was **published** in the USA. It was an instant hit with children and within a month all 10,000 copies printed had been sold.

Patricia Neal with Paul Newman in the film *Hud*. She won an Academy Award (Oscar) for best actress for her work in this film.

What the readers say

Children in the USA say what they think about *Charlie*:

'Your mouths will water with delight!'
(Trevor, age 8 and Jonah, age 9, from New York)

'Parents, you should buy this book for all of your children...'
(Justin, age 10, from Carmel, California)

Another tragedy

In February 1965, when Pat was expecting another baby, she suddenly collapsed with bleeding in her brain. She was rushed to hospital, but was left unable to walk or talk. Roald was shattered. He moved the family back to the quiet and privacy of Gipsy House and designed a special programme of exercises to help Pat get better. Fortunately, baby Lucy was born safely in August.

Hooray for Hollywood!

While Pat was ill and could not work, Roald tried to earn more money by writing film scripts instead of books. These included the James Bond film *You Only Live Twice*, the children's movie *Chitty Chitty Bang Bang* and a movie of *Charlie and the Chocolate Factory*. But Roald hated working as a team with directors, producers and other writers. As Pat slowly recovered, he gladly returned to his own stories.

▲ A scene from the film about a flying car, *Chitty Chitty Bang Bang*.

James and Charlie hit Britain

By 1966, *James* and *Charlie* were still not published in Britain. Roald had sent them both to all the leading **publishers**, but they had turned the stories down. **Editors** thought the tales were rude and violent and contained jokes that only adults would understand. Then one day, one of Tessa's friends borrowed the US copies to read at home. Her father, who was a publisher, saw the books and asked to meet Roald. In 1967, copies were at last in British bookshops and libraries, flying off the shelves.

Wonderful or worthless?

Some Americans agreed with those in Britain who thought that Roald's ideas were dangerous and not suitable for children. For instance, certain **critics** thought it was scary to have aunties being squashed to death under a giant peach!

In 1970 a big row broke out in the USA over whether *Charlie* showed white people in power over black people. The pictures showed black Oompa Loompas working like slaves for the white Willy Wonka. Roald was horrified. He agreed to have the pictures changed so that they no longer looked like black people.

▲ *Charlie and the Chocolate Factory*, which was finally published in Britain in 1967.

In the middle of all the fuss, Roald's new story for very young children was brought out – *Fantastic Mr Fox*. Roald's publishers were worried that people might say it encouraged children to steal. Fortunately it was another instant best-seller.

▲ By the time the film of *Charlie* was made, the row about the Oompa Loompas had died down.

What a reviewer said

When *Charlie and the Chocolate Factory* was finally published in Britain, Elaine Moss – a book critic for *The Times* newspaper – said that it was *'the funniest book I have read in years'*.

Fame and fortune

For a while, Roald seemed to run out of ideas. He wrote a follow-up to *Charlie and the Chocolate Factory*, called *Charlie and the Great Glass Elevator*, and turned an earlier story into *Danny, the Champion of the World*. Perhaps Roald found it difficult to write new tales because he was unhappy. His wartime wounds were causing him a lot of pain and making him very irritable. He was quarrelling with his **publishers** over money and ideas. Worst of all, he and Pat were no longer getting on.

A perfect partnership

The turning point for Roald's writing came when he struck up a new working relationship. An illustrator called Quentin Blake drew the pictures for Roald's new book, *The Enormous Crocodile*

(1978), followed by *The Twits* (1980) and *George's Marvellous Medicine* (1981). Quentin's illustrations 'softened' the nastiness that some people said existed in Roald's stories. *The BFG*, illustrated by Quentin and **published** in 1982, was a huge hit.

The book illustrator, Quentin Blake, holding one of his illustrations.

▲ Quentin's illustration of the tall, thin Roald Dahl. It makes him look like a BFG!

Changes

In 1983, Roald and Pat sadly **divorced**. Roald was 67 years old, but he married a long-time friend, Felicity Crosland. In his new happiness, he wrote more fantastic stories, such as *The Witches* and *Matilda*. Millions of children all over the world loved Roald as their all-time favourite author.

What Roald said

Roald once said about Quentin Blake:

'It is Quent's pictures rather than my own written descriptions that have brought to life such characters as the BFG.'

Roald Dahl on Roald Dahl

Roald received over 500 letters a week from readers, wanting to find out about his life and work. Here are some of the things he said in the many interviews he gave to magazines and on radio and TV programmes.

On his job:
'One of the nice things about being a writer is that all you need is what you've got in your head, and a pencil and a bit of paper.'

On writing for children:
'The job of a children's writer is to try to write a book that is so exciting and fast and wonderful that the child falls in love with it.'

On being famous:
'I suppose I could knock at the door of any house where there was a child – whether it was the US, Britain, Holland, Germany, France … and they'd know me. That does make me feel good.'

How Roald worked

Roald wrote in a shed at the bottom of the garden at Gipsy House. He sat in an old armchair, with his legs in a sleeping bag, resting his feet on a case. He leaned on a large, flat board resting across the arms of the chair and wrote with a pencil on yellow paper. Roald worked six or seven days a week, from 10 a.m. until lunchtime and 4 p.m. until 6 p.m. in the afternoon. He was a slow worker. A short story for grown ups took four to six months. A story for children took between six months and a year. Roald did not go out looking for things to write about. He once said, 'My ideas occur basically at my desk.'

On putting 'whizzpops' in The BFG:
'There is nothing that makes a child laugh more than an adult suddenly farting in a room.'

On violence in his books:
'Children know that the violence in my books is only make believe. It's much like the violence in the old fairy tales ... These tales are pretty rough, but the violence is confined to a magical time and place.'

On complaints about bad taste in his stories:
'I never get any protests from children ... I know what children like.'

▲ Roald at work in his shed at the bottom of the Gipsy House garden.

A man with 'child power'

Roald enjoyed meeting his fans. He endlessly visited bookshops and libraries, and travelled on book tours to many different countries. He adored being well-known and loved by children. He once called it having 'child power'! However, he always felt that adult **critics** did not like his work as much as they should. Roald was given an important award, called the Whitbread Prize, in 1983 for *The Witches*. He thought that his work should have won an award sooner! He also felt he deserved to be made 'Sir Roald Dahl'. In 1987, Roald was offered a less important honour, the **OBE**. He refused to accept it.

Growing grumpy

As an elderly man, Roald was very grumpy with grown-ups. He often caused arguments and offended people. He was perhaps so irritable because his health was growing worse and worse. In 1990, when he was 74, his love story for very young children was **published**. It was called *Esio Trot*. Later that year, on 23 November, Roald died of illness.

Roald's grave is in the churchyard at Great Missenden, not far from Gipsy House. 'Footprints' in the grass lead from a beach down to the grave.

Most bookshops have several shelves of books by Roald Dahl, who continues to be one of the most popular children's writers.

Not 'The End'

The last two tales Roald ever wrote were published after he died. *The Vicar of Nibbleswicke* is a story about a young vicar who gets into trouble for saying words back-to-front, such as 'dog' for 'god', and 'krap' for 'park'! Roald's final story was *The Minpins*, a fairytale in which a boy helps some dwarf-like creatures get rid of a fire-breathing monster.

Yet children all over the world still longed for more. Roald's **publishers** brought out collections of rhymes and recipes from his stories. Fans set up Dahl clubs and websites. Roald's books continue to be best-sellers today.

A friend to all children

Roald always remained very thoughtful and kind to children. He gave his £3000 Whitbread Prize money to a hospice for dying children. He bought equipment for disabled children, supported projects to raise money for children's hospitals, and helped with any government plans that encouraged children to read.

Timeline

1916 Roald Dahl is born

1938 Sent to Africa to work for Shell in Dar-es-Salaam, Tanzania

1939 Joins the **Royal Air Force** to fight in **World War II**

1942 Sent in January to work in the British **Embassy**, Washington

1942 In August first adult story is **published** – *Shot Down Over Libya*

1943 First children's book is published – *The Gremlins*

1953 Marries Patricia Neal, with whom he has a son and four daughters

1978 Partnership with Quentin Blake begins with publication of *The Enormous Crocodile*

1983 Roald and Pat **divorce**. Roald marries Felicity Crosland. Roald wins the Whitbread Prize for *The Witches*

1990 Roald dies

Books by Roald Dahl

Here are some of the many books written by Roald Dahl:

James and the Giant Peach (first published in 1961)
An orphan boy escapes from two cruel aunts and travels the world with a group of human-sized insects inside a huge, magical peach.

Charlie and the Chocolate Factory (first published in 1964)
A poor boy called Charlie Bucket wins a tour around a fantastic, top-secret chocolate factory, with some rather unpleasant children and their equally unpleasant parents.

The BFG (first published in 1982)
An orphan called Sophie meets a Big Friendly Giant whose friends are in the habit of eating children. Together, they set out to try and stop the bad giants...

Glossary

baptized made a member of the church

blackout when you lose the ability to see, think, talk and move for a few moments

boarding school school where pupils stay and live during term-time, only going home in the holidays

characters people in a story

cockpit part of the aeroplane where the pilot sits

critic person who is paid to read a story and write their opinion of it

divorce legal process, in which a marriage is officially ended

editor person in a publishing company whose job is to work with an author to make the author's writing as good as possible

embassy office that the government of one country has in another country

film script story and words for a film

homesick when somebody feels upset because they are living away from home and they miss their home and family very much

hospice special hospital for dying people

inspiration influence or encouragement to do something

Norwegian person from the country of Norway

OBE medal awarded by the Queen called the Order of the British Empire. It is given to people who have done important or outstanding things.

published when someone's writing is printed in a book or a newspaper or magazine article

publisher person or company that makes and sells books

Royal Air Force (RAF) Britain has three military services: the RAF, who fight in planes in the air; the navy, who fight in boats and submarines at sea; and the army, who fight on land

ship-broker person who supplies a ship with everything it needs when it comes into port (such as fuel, food and tools)

World War II war (1939–45) that began when Germany invaded Poland

Index

Titles in the *All About Authors* series are:

All about...
Malorie Blackman

Shaun McCarthy

Hardback   0 431 17982 4

All about...
Roald Dahl

Vic Parker

Hardback   0 431 17981 6

All about...
J.K. Rowling

Shaun McCarthy

Hardback   0 431 17980 8

All about...
Jacqueline Wilson

Vic Parker

Hardback   0 431 17983 2

Find out about the other titles in this series on our website www.heinemann.co.uk/library